A note from the heart

In gratitude and grace

First to Almighty God, who gave me a brain,
to write through the sunshine, the joy, and the pain.

Big thanks to Jerilee (Myah), my editor in chief and technical support and art & design guide,

She stepped in right on time to stand by my side.
Helping me format each picture and line,
Her help put these pages together with pride.

To Heather, who cheered every word I've penned,
Encouraging every step from beginning to end,
Giving me the push to make my poems known.

To Azul and Anthony, for each silent thumbs up,
Your quiet inspiration keeps filling my cup.
"Mommy, it sounds better if you say this instead,"
"Yeah, it sounds good," Anthony said with a nod of his head.

To my sisters and Mom, my family, my team,
Thank you for lifting me high with each dream.
Day after day, you hold up my heart,
Guiding my steps right from the start.

And to you, dear readers, as you put down your pen,
May your souls be refreshed again and again.

SHE IS
Strong
Myah'sPocket

Chapter 1

The Weight and The Relief

Mindfulness & Letting Go

Your Mental Weight

By Sandia Williams Whyte

It’s not in my bones, it’s behind my eyes
A tired that sleep won’t apologize.
Eight hours down, still I wake unmade,
Like my mind ran miles while my body stayed.

Water’s a whisper. Rest feels like lies.
One email, one text, and my focus dies.
This kind of tired isn’t chased by night;
It’s a fog that swallows morning light.

So I press cold to my face, count breath to ten,
Let the ice remind me how to begin again.
I spill every thought onto paper, bare,
Don’t fix, don’t hold, just set them there.

I look far off when the screen burns near,
Give my eyes the distance they beg for here.
And I name it plain: "Overloaded, not weak,”
Because shame is the thief that makes the tired speak.

This isn’t failing. It’s a white flag drawn.
So I rest without guilt till the fog moves on.

1 Peter 5:7

"Cast all your anxiety on him because he cares for you."

Guided Journaling Prompt:

What is the heaviest thought taking up space in your mind today? Write it down plainly below, then consciously hand it over to God, asking Him to replace that heavy weight with His perfect peace.

BREATHE

Fat

By Sandia Williams Whyte

Fat, fat, fat,
look at that.
Fat on my arms,
fat on my back.
Fat on my tummy,
fat on my thighs.
Fat in places
that surprise my eyes.

I try to hide it,
I try to squeeze,
but it always finds a way
to cause unease.

They say "just exercise,"
they say "just eat right,"
but it's a constant battle,
a daily fight.

But then I remember,
I am more than my size.
I am beautifully made
in my Creator's eyes.

So fat, fat, fat,
you can stay right there,
because my worth is not found
in the clothes that I wear.

Psalm 139:14

"I praise you because I am fearfully and wonderfully made; your works are wonderful, I know that full well."

Guided Journaling Prompt:

Society tells us how our bodies "should" look, but God says you are already a masterpiece. Write down three things you love about yourself that have absolutely nothing to do with your physical appearance.

Pain

By Sandia Williams Whyte

Pain, pain, go away,
don't come back another day.

You hurt my body, you hurt my mind,
you leave my joy far behind.

You make me cry, you make me scream,
you shatter every single dream.

You are a visitor I did not invite,
who keeps me awake all through the night.

But in my pain, I find a strength,
to go to any kind of length.

To look for hope, to look for light,
to keep on pushing through the night.

For pain is just a temporary thing,
and joy is what tomorrow will bring.

Revelation 21:14

"He will wipe every tear from their eyes. There will be no more death or mourning or crying or pain, for the old order of things has passed away."

Guided Journaling Prompt:

Pain can feel like a thief that never leaves. Write about a time in your past where you walked through a painful season, but eventually found joy or strength on the other side. Let it remind you that this current pain will pass too.

Thunder Storm Sleep

By Sandia Williams Whyte

Klash! Buum! Pow!

A Scream, a Shout, a Shake, a Shiver

A hug, a squeeze, a mind at ease.

It's O.K. don't be Afraid
I am here I'll hold you near.

A Cry, a Tear, I Can see your fear.
It's alright I'll stay with you tonight.

A Smile, a Chuckle, a giggle, a wiggle
As you are tickled,

We play and play we're O.k.
Tip Tip faster
Pita Pata Pita Pata faster

Oh ooo it O.K. Lighting,
Thunder, no need to fear no
need to Wonder.

Rain Ahhh....

Quiet.....

Sleep....

Psalm 4:8

"In peace I will lie down and sleep, for you alone, Lord, make me dwell in safety."

Guided Journaling Prompt:

Sandia beautifully illustrates how a terrifying storm can turn into a peaceful sleep when we are held tight by someone who loves us. What "thunder" or loud anxiety is roaring in your life right now? Write it down, imagine Jesus wrapping you in a safe hug, and telling you to rest.

Chapter 2

The Anchor

Deep Faith & God's Presence

The Four Kinds of Light

By Sandia Williams Whyte

The Four Kinds of Light
that shine so bright.

The sun, the moon, the stars,
and the light that is within us.

The sun that shines by day,
to guide us on our way.

The moon that shines by night,
to give us a beautiful sight.

The stars that twinkle up high,
like diamonds in the sky.

But the greatest light of all,
is the one that answers our call.

The light that burns inside,
where Holy Spirit does reside.

It guides us through the dark,
and leaves a beautiful mark.

So let your inner light shine,
and everything will be just fine.

Psalm 4:8

"In the same way, let your light shine before others, that they may see your good deeds and glorify your Father in heaven."

Guided Journaling Prompt:

Your inner light is fueled by the Holy Spirit. Who is someone in your life who needs you to share your light, encouragement, or kindness with them this week? Write down their name and what you can do for them.

I Have No Man

By Sandia Williams Whyte

Broken, crippled, unable to move. Looking around for an outstretched hand: just to say, "I am Here I have a plan. Many years have passed with little progress, many pass me but why?
My answer is, "I have no man". No man to help, no man to lift me to the pool of mercy, no man to carry me to the waters of grace. No man to assist me to get my healing.

But wait, I've been looking in the wrong place.
As I lay on my bed, my mat of comfort. Remaining in the same position, waiting for some kind man to assist my situation.

I heard a voice, it said, "do you want healing"? But my answer was, I have no man, No man to assist me in the pool of mercy. No man to carry me to the water of grace.
But he never pointed me to Bethesda
for he knows there was no healing there.

He never looked at my excuses or listened to whom I blamed.
He knew that blaming others had become our nature. All he did was make a command. He said, "get up, stand up, pick up, take up your bed and walk!"

To him, there was no reason for me not to get my healing,
His command gave me strength to move on.
His command said it all.
Yes! So I got up, I stood up, I picked up and I walked.

Today, the I have no man excuse, is not for me.
I have a man who is unlike any man. He has power over every situation. Every brokenness, every crippling circumstance.
My man is a healer, sustainer, provider, protector, saviour, and friend.
He promised never to leave me or forsake me.
Now I boldly say" I Have A Man!"
I have a man, His name is Jesus.

Isaiah 54:5

"For your Maker is your husband—the Lord Almighty is his name—the Holy One of Israel is your Redeemer; he is called the God of all the earth."

Guided Journaling Prompt:

Human relationships are wonderful, but they can fail us. God's presence, however, is an unbreakable anchor. Reflect on the areas where you feel lonely or misunderstood. Write a prayer asking God to fill those spaces completely.

I AM PROTECTED BY GOD

I Am Here

By Sandia Williams Whyte

I am here,
don't you fear.

I am here,
wipe that tear.

I am here,
draw me near.

I am here,
loud and clear.

These are the words my Father spoke,
when my heavy spirit broke.

He held me close, He held me tight,
and turned my darkness into light.

He said "My child, I'll never leave,
just trust in Me and just believe.

I am your shield, I am your tower,
I will give you strength and power."

So now I stand and do not shake,
because of the promise He did make.

Deuteronomy 31:6

"Be strong and courageous. Do not be afraid or terrified because of them, for the Lord your God goes with you; he will never leave you nor forsake you."

Imagine the Lord standing right next to you, looking at your current situation, and saying, "I am here, don't you fear." What fears melt away when you remember that the Creator of the universe is shielding you? Write them down and let them go.

Guided Journaling Prompt:

Consistently Constant

By Sandia Williams Whyte

Consistently Constant
That's you.
When things are good you are there through and through.

When things are bad you are there even more, true.
When the sun is high and my days are bright,
You are there being that light.

When clouds are around and the rains fall down,
And everywhere seems dark, no hope, no light, no way out;
You are there holding me tight.
Carrying me through the darkness into your light.
Telling me, "My child, I'm here, don't you fear.
I will never leave you shattered and scared.

I am the Potter, remember to me you are clay.
Let me mold you and make you, my child, today.

Lean on me when all your strength is gone,
I will carry you on and on.

Depend on me without shame or scorn,
I'm here for you, let me carry you through.

Don't fight me child, my love is true,
And there is nothing that you can do.
Because I am consistently and constantly here for you.

I gave up my life, my blood just for you.
It's a price I paid willingly for you.

It's a gift, no need to twitch.
You don't need to work and pay me back for it.

Just be obedient, faithful and true.
Trust me child, because I love you."

Isaiah 64:8

"Yet you, Lord, are our Father. We are the clay, you are the potter; we are all the work of your hand."

Guided Journaling Prompt:

Sandia writes about a God who is consistently constant, even when our circumstances change like the weather. It can be exhausting trying to "earn" love, but God's grace is a free gift. What areas of your life are you struggling to control right now? Write them down, and practice letting the Potter mold your situation

Promise and Praise

By Sandia Williams Whyte

A promise made, a promise kept,
while the weary world softly slept.

He promised peace, He promised grace,
to everyone in every place.

So I will lift my voice and praise,
through all of my remaining days.

I'll praise Him in the morning light,
I'll praise Him in the darkest night.

For He has broken every chain,
and washed away my deepest stain.

My lips will shout, my heart will sing,
unto my Savior and my King.

Psalm 145:2

"Every day I will praise you and extol your name for ever and ever."

Guided Journaling Prompt:

Praise changes our perspective. Even if you are waiting on a breakthrough, what are 5 specific promises or blessings God has already given you that you can praise Him for right now?

What Is THIS?!

By Sandia Williams Whyte

Jesus walk in, look all around

He starts to teach a brand new sound! Not
like the rest, His voice so strong
People say WOW! all day long!

Everybody shout
What is THIS?!
What is THIS?!

Jesus teaches with AUTHORITY Even bad
spirits say Oh me! and flee!

Him say Come out! just one time
Bad spirits run, don't waste no time!
People watch, dem eyes go wide
His words have POWER! Everybody cried!

Everybody shout
What is THIS?!
What is THIS?!

Jesus teaches with AUTHORITY!
Even bad spirits say Oh me! and flee!

When Jesus speaks... Things change!
When Jesus speaks... Fear runs away! What is
THIS?! A NEW DAY!

Mark 1:27-28

"they were all so amazed that they asked each other, What is this? A new teaching and with authority! he even gives orders to impure spirits and they obey him. News about him spread quickly over the whole region of galilee."

Guided Journaling Prompt:

What fear or heavy situation in your life do you need Jesus to speak authority over today? Write it down, and ask Him to bring His peace into that space.

Chapter 3

Sweet Symphony

Love, Family & Sisterhood

My True Blue

By Sandia Williams Whyte

Azul, my Az, my Zul, my A.R.,
My True Blue, my blessing, my shining star.
Have I told you, son, that I love you so?
More than you see, more than you know.

When I see your face and when you're away,
My heart still says your name each day.
I pray for you when I'm on my knees,
And when I'm quiet in the rustling trees.
God's my go-to when it's you I bring,
'Cause you belong to the Heavenly King.

You're my heir to hope and faith and light,
No flaw, no fall could change that right.
You'll never be a disappointment, son,
You're my blessing, my chosen one.

I love you more than words can say,
May blessings chase you through your day.
May your desires be met, and more air
Fill your lungs with joy and prayer.

Wear kindness daily, make it yours,
Let love be what your heart adores.
And when the world gets loud and wild,
I pray you hear Him, gentle and mild.

Science calls it inferring, you see
Believing truth you cannot see.
That's how I trust, and that's how you'll grow,
Knowing the One who loves you so.

Jesus is your Friend, He knows your name,
He knows your heart better than you can claim.
Don't neglect that bond, hold it tight,
He walks with you through day and night.

From the top of your hair to your dancing feet,
Fast as a hare, quick and fleet
Run to the life He's planned for you,
My son, my blessing, my True Blue.

So be safe today, and always know:
My love for you will never slow.
More than I can ever tell,
Az, I love you, all is well

Psalm 127 :3

Children are a heritage from the Lord offspring a reward from him.

Guided Journaling Prompt:

Children and loved ones are pure gifts from heaven. Write a specific letter of blessing or a prayer of protection for your child or a loved one today. expressing your deepest hopes for their life and future.

I Love You

By Sandia Williams Whyte

I love you
I love your eyes,
they look like skies.
I love the way you eat,
I love the way you sleep.

I love your chin,
I love your grin.
I love the way you make me spin
when you move like the wind.

I love your hair,
I love your ear.
I love the fact that you don't care,
I love the way you love to share.

I love your vest and how you sit at your desk, I love the way that you get dressed, I love the fact you make a mess.

I love your nose,
I love your toes,
I love the way you strike a pose.
After You Steal Grandma's Rose

I love your sneeze,
"Excuse me, please."
I love the way you scratch your knees.

I love your walk,
I love your talk.
I love the fact that you're smart,
I love to take you to the park.

I love your laugh,
I love your cough,
I love your smile.
I love the way you drive me wild,
I love your style.
I love the fact that you're my child.

I could not love you more, and yet
I love the way you make me bubble.
I love the fact that you give trouble.

I love that you're such a sneak,
and wake Grandpa when he's asleep.

I love the fact that you are tall.
I can remember when you were small.

I loved your shoe,
I loved your coo.
I love the fact that this is you.
I love your little blue.
Please stay just as true.

I'll do all I can do,
because I love you.

Love you, Azul.
For my blue and red,
which makes a perfect colour purple.

Proverbs 17:6

Children's children are a crown to the aged, and parents are the pride of their children."

Guided Journaling Prompt:

Sandia writes a beautiful, detailed list of all the quirky, messy, and joyful reasons she loves her child - even that he gives trouble

Reflect on your family. Write down a list of the little, everyday habits or traits you love about them.

My Sisters in Beautiful Bloom

By Sandia Williams Whyte

You're the sisters I cherish, a gift so divine,
Amoy, Heather, Mona, Jeri, Brandie, you shine.

Supportive and encouraging, honest and true,
You show me Christ's love, and I'm blessed anew.
You laugh with me, at me, in joyful gime,
Reminding me I'm loved, and I'm never alone in time.

You celebrate my wins, big or small,
Genuine happiness, love that stands tall.
You've taught me to bloom, to find my own way,
And when I struggled, you showed me the day.

Like mastering a braid, you stood by me,
Cheering me on, till I got it free.

Mona, you've combed my hair, through trials and fun,
Teaching me patience, and loving me, one braid at a time, you've begun.

Jeri, your listening ear, and scripture-filled heart,
Have helped me navigate life, and never had to depart

Brandie, your honesty, and upfront love,
Have kept me grounded, and guided me from above.

Heather, your support, and encouragement true,
Point me to God, and remind me of His love anew

Amoy, you've been my safe haven, my partner in crime,
Patiently keeping up with my antics and rhymes.

You've shown me God's love, in all that you do,
And I'm grateful, sis, for each one of you.

You help me bloom where I'm planted, grow,
Reminding me of God's guide, my light, my way to go.

You tell me who I am, and to whom I belong,
I belong to Jesus, and in Him, I sing my song.

Ecclesiastes 4:12

"Though one may be overpowered, two can defend themselves. A cord of three strands is not quickly broken."

Guided Journaling Prompt:

Sisterhood and healthy friendships are essential for our growth. Take a moment to think about the women or friends who stand by you. Write down their names and a short note of gratitude for how they help you "bloom" in life.

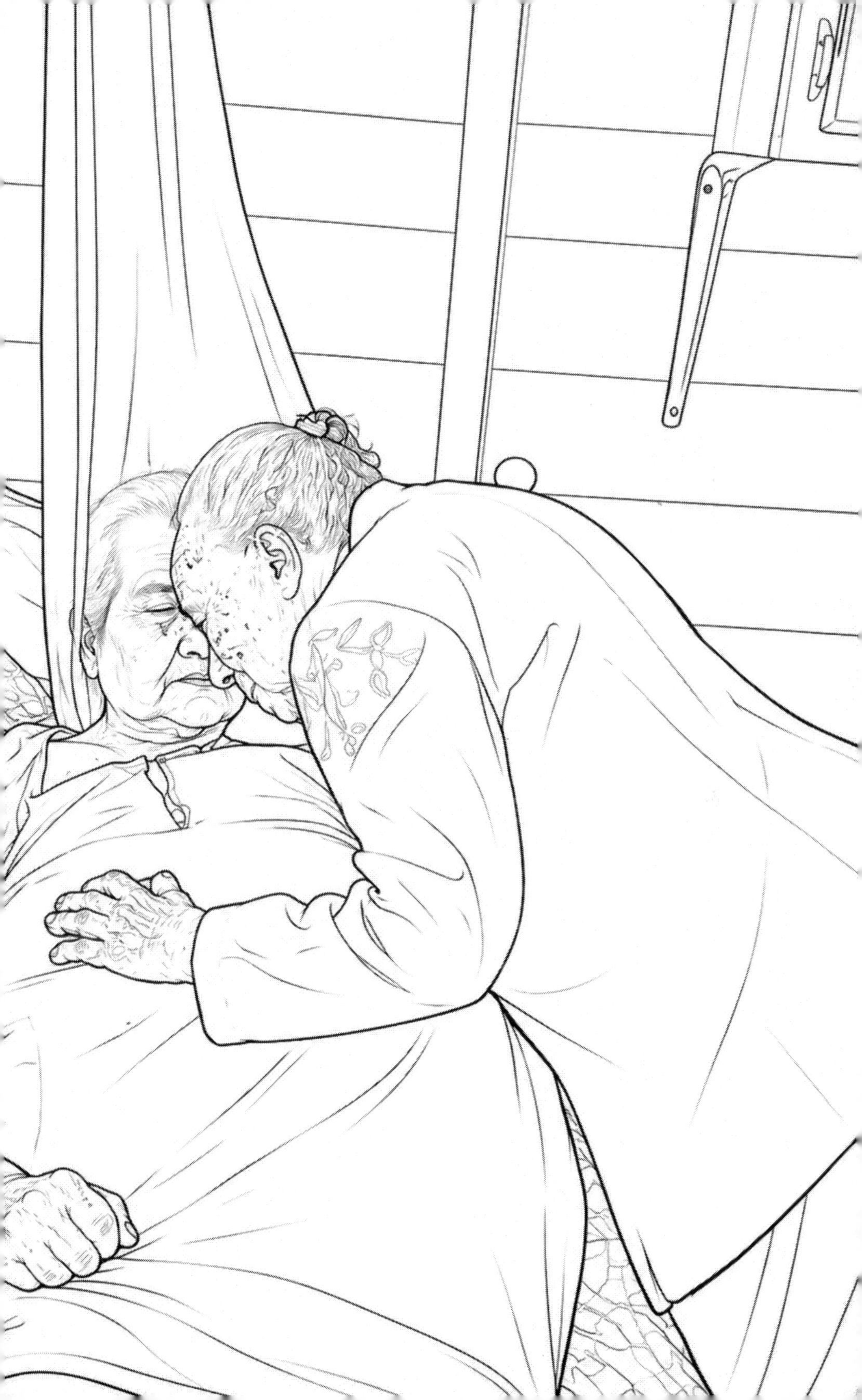

The Loudest Hug

By Sandia Williams Whyte

Forehead to forehead, white against pink,
no words were spoken, but the silence would think.

Two sisters met where the years had been long,
and in that embrace, they both found their song.

It whispered I see you. It whispered I'm near.
It whispered we're two now, but the love's still here.
It said you are home, and it said you are known,
and for one quiet moment, you were never alone.

Warmth met with warmth, and the past drifted near.
Years of love, years of knowing, held crystal clear.
Sister to sister, bond strong and true,
The hug said it all, for me and for you.

No words could hold it, no time could erase
Love saw it all in that single embrace.

Romans 12:15

"Rejoice with those who rejoice; mourn with those who mourn."

Guided Journaling Prompt:

A physical hug or a moment of silent comfort can communicate love better than words ever could. Think about a time someone gave you comfort when you were down. How can you be a comforting, safe presence for someone else today?

Love

By Sandia Williams Whyte

Love is patient, love is kind,
the greatest treasure you can find. It
doesn't envy, doesn't boast,
it loves the ones who need it most.

It covers faults, it heals the sore,
it opens up the tightest door.
It never fails, it never ends,
It makes the broken pieces friends

So let love rule, let love guide,
and cast all bitter pride aside

For love is God and God is love,
descending softly like a dove

1 Corinthians 13: 4-7

Love is patient, love is kind. It does not envy , it does not boast,it is not proud... it always protect, always trust,always hopes,always preserves.

Guided Journaling Prompt:

The Bible says that love is an action, not just a feeling. Which characteristic of love (patience, kindness, humility, forgiveness) do you need to practice more intentionally in your life right now? Write about how you can apply it.

Chapter 4

Island Joy & Real Talk

Humor, Culture & Reality

Lash Dem A Come

By Sandia Williams Whyte

Big girl, slim girl, tall girl, small,
Is lashes a run di place, watch dem all!
Yuh see di lash before yuh see di face,
No matter di size, dem a lead di race!

BAP! BAP! Two blink breeze start blow,
Fan? Who need fan? Dem a di star, a di show!
AC nah necessary, di lash a flex,
Hurricane a come? Dem nah move nex'!

Sunscreen? Where? Don't even check dat,
Di lash dem cast shade pan yuh neck back!
UV cyah touch yuh, yuh safe an' bless,
Mongoose a hide when di lash dem press!

Mi seh di lash dem have VIP pass,
Walk inna di room everybody gasp!
Not "Hey girl" is "Hey LASH"dem shout,
Di girl a come after, still walking out!

So fat or slim, short or tall,
Once di lash deh pan yuh wall,
Yuh ready fi road, yuh ready fi stall,
Two blink cool down — yuh breeze through all!

BAP! BAP!

1 Samuel 16 :7

For the Lord sees not as man sees: man looks on the outward appearance, but the Lord looks on the heart."

Guided Journaling Prompt:

Your confidence is so bright that it makes everyone in the room stop and take notice! What is one unique quality or trait God gave you that always stands out?

Write down how you will embrace this strength today and move forward with total confidence.

PhD from the University of...
"Me Did Have it Too"

By Sandia Williams Whyte

You ever notice,
Most Jamaican family fren,
'Specially di elderly dem
Dem have PhD inna DIAGNOSIS!

You pon di phone,
Dem voice so sweet:
"How yuh duh, bwoy?
Yuh alright, sweet?"

You say:
"Bwoy mi alright,
Just a likkle pain inna mi BACK."

BAM!
Consultation start!
No appointment,
No chart!

"A NERVE dat, yuh nuh!
Cause mi did a suffer from it TOO!
Or a GAS, man!
Mi did have dat last WEEK;
Just drink some ginger TEA!"

"Woi, mi ELBOW!
Lawks, yuh a get ARTHRITIS too?"

Mi haffi ask
Weh dem go study?
What med school dem attend?
When dem graduate, my friend?

Cause dem nuh need no class, no book, no certificate
Dem graduate from "Me Did Have It Too" University!

Class of Every Week, Doctor of Everybody Business an' dem never even pay fi sit di test!

Proverbs 18:2

"Fools find no pleasure in understanding but delight in airing their own opinions."

Guided Journaling Prompt:

This poem uses wonderful humor to highlight how exhausting it can be when people constantly try to "one-up" our experiences. How do you handle people who try to steal your joy or overshadow your stories? Reflect on how to protect your peace with a smile.

You Just Pretty Suh!

By Sandia Williams Whyte

You just pretty suh, pretty suh, yes you!
Your smile shine bright, it light up the room.
Your warmth and your aura, your spirit too,
God did a good work when Him fashion you.

You a God-bless pickney, full of love and truth,
His spirit a live right there in you.

From your heart to your eyes, the joy run through, Everywhere you go, blessings follow you.

You just pretty suh, pretty suh, that's true!
Not just on the outside, but deep down too.

Your light sweet, your soul sweet, through and through, The whole world can see, you just pretty suh, a true!

Psalm 139:14

"praise you because I am fearfully and wonderfully made; your works are wonderful, I know that fully well."

Guided Journaling Prompt:

This poem reminds us that true beauty is engineered by God and shines from a sweet soul. Looking in the mirror, it's easy to focus on flaws. Write down three things about your inner spirit, your aura, or your heart that make you "pretty suh" in the eyes of God.

Love's Empty Sea

By Sandia Williams Whyte

Trust breaks, love fades away,
Words unsaid, hearts in disarray.
Money fights, distance grows,
Intimacy lost, love's last pose.
Respect fades, love's flame dies,
Couples drift, and goodbye replies.

Forgiveness scarce, grudges held tight,
Disrespect whispered, through the night.
Infidelity's sting, a wound so deep,
Love's foundation starts to crumble and creep.
Priorities misplaced, God's forgotten name,
Couples lost, in a loveless game.

Spiritually lost, in their own haze,
They forget the One who guides their ways.
God at the center, the missing key,
Without Him, love's just an empty sea.
Selfish dreams, and ego's pride,
Lead to broken hearts, and a love that die.

Psalm 147:3

"He heals the brokenhearted and binds up their wounds."

Guided Journaling Prompt:

Human love can sometimes leave us feeling empty, like looking out at a barren shore. If you have experienced a disappointment in romance or friendship, write about what lessons you learned that made you stronger and wiser.

Kissing Me Lastnight

By Sandia Williams Whyte

You were kissing me last night,
under de yellow streetlamp light.

Sweet talk flowing like a stream,
making me feel like it's a dream.

But morning come and de light did change, and suddenly you acting strange.

De sweet talk gone, de temperature cold,
not a single hand for me to hold.

So keep your kisses, keep your game,
you won't catch me in dis trap again.

Me value meself way too high,
to settle for a temporary guy.

Proverbs 4:23

"Above all else, guard your heart, for everything you do flows from it."

Guided Journaling Prompt:

Guarding your heart means refusing to accept inconsistent, "temporary" love. What boundaries do you need to put in place to guard your heart, your energy, and your peace from people who aren't serious about valuing you?

Reader's Bonus Section

My Own Song

Use this beautiful blank space to write out your own verses, songs, thougths or prayers. Let your soul speak.

Made in the USA
Monee, IL
12 November 2026

f6b69e4c-47c6-4287-97f3-6456257b1f05R01